BOOKS, BOOKS, BOOKS

BOOKS, BOOKS, BOOKS

A Hilarious Collection of Literary Cartoons

**edited by
S. Gross and Jim Charlton**

HARPER & ROW, PUBLISHERS, New York
Cambridge, Philadelphia, San Francisco
London, Mexico City, São Paulo, Singapore, Sydney

1817

Grateful acknowledgement is made for permission to reprint:

Cartoon on page 6 by Brian Savage by *Playboy.* Copyright 1969 by *Playboy.* Reproduced by special permission of *Playboy* Magazine.

Cartoons copyrighted by *The New Yorker* are indicated throughout the book.

FIRST EDITION

Designed by Hudson Studio

LIBRARY OF CONGRESS CATALOG CARD NUMBER: 88-45172
ISBN: 0-06-016004-7

88 89 90 91 92 HOR 10 9 8 7 6 5 4 3 2 1

JOHN JONIK

"For a brief moment I thought we were witnessing
the bright new dawn of a literary renaissance."

BRIAN SAVAGE

FROM MAY D. FARNSWORTH'S
"RUNAWAY" SERIES

May D. Farnsworth's

THE RUNAWAY BUTTON

Tim Button jumps off a pajama top during the spin cycle. What happens next?

May D. Farnsworth's

The Runaway Umbrella

Carl Umbrella is sick of belonging to a certain person, so he makes a break for it. What will the outcome be?

May D. Farnsworth's

THE RUNAWAY CHEAP BALL-POINT PEN

Lester Cheap Ball-Point Pen escapes from a salesman's desk. What follows is anybody's guess!

R. Chast

ROZ CHAST

ROGET'S BOOK OF WORDS THAT MEAN THE SAME THING AS OTHER WORDS, OR ALMOST THE SAME THING.

JOHN JONIK

HENRY MARTIN

DEAN VIETOR

© 1983 The New Yorker Magazine, Inc.

"Well, it's good, but people just don't write books all by themselves anymore."

"It's $37.50 until December 31. Thereafter $50.00, and to some people we might not sell it at any price."

ELDON DEDINI

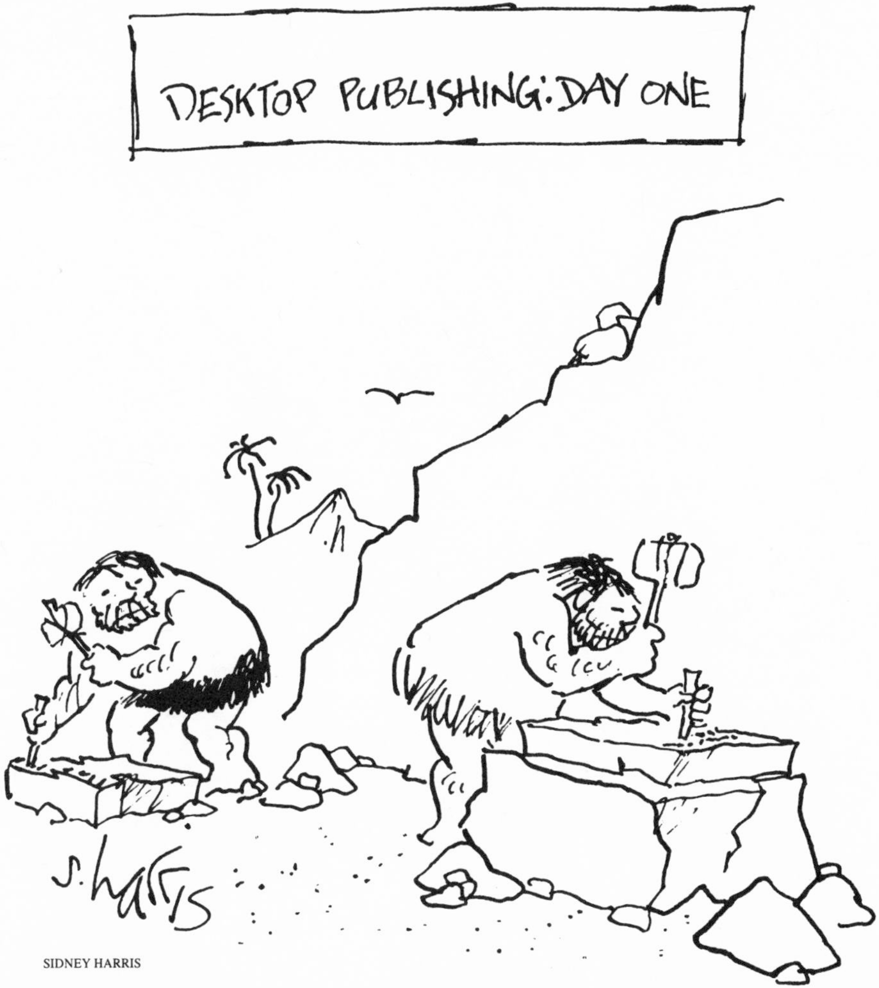

SIDNEY HARRIS

"Damn it! Wait your turn!"

BILL WOODMAN

ELDON DEDINI

"I just love it when you quote Blake."

EDWARD FRASCINO

SIPRESS

DAVID SIPRESS

"You don't know me but I'm writing your biography."

BILL PLYMPTON

Word Processor

JOSEPH MIRACHI

"This is it, Myra. I'm going out for a shave and a haircut and then I begin writing trash."

S.GROSS

SAM GROSS

BORIS DRUCKER

DICK OLDDEN

WARREN MILLER

© 1982 The New Yorker Magazine, Inc.

"Sorry I'm late, just couldn't put your book down."

BERNARD SCHOENBAUM

"We'd do him a big favor if we ate chapter four."

CATHERINE SIRACUSA

SECOND NOVEL

EDWARD FRASCINO

"I recited the *Kama Sutra* to lots of dames. You were the only one who fell for it."

HENRY MARTIN

"A Mr. Squirrel Nutkin and a Mrs. Tiggywinkle are here to see you."

"Holy cow! What kind of crazy people used to live here anyway?"

WARREN MILLER

CATHARINE O'NEILL

TIME
10:45

TEMP
68°

NUMBER OF WRITERS
WHOSE MOTHERS
KEEP SAYING:
"SO WHEN ARE
YOU GOING TO
GET A JOB?"

22,743

RICHARD ORLIN

ARNOLDO FRANCHIONI

LARRY BARTH

"This had better be good, Robinson!"

CHARLES ADDAMS

THE ISLAND OF LOST MANUSCRIPTS

OLIVER CHRISTIANSON (REVILO)

On April 12, 1986, Arland T. Dufresne accidently
hits the "Global Delete" button while
typing the last paragraph of his 1026 page novel.

THOMAS CHENEY

"The vermouth is over the refrigerator.
That's my novel."

CHARLES SAXON

© 1980 The New Yorker Magazine, Inc.

"Sorry, but all our business success books have been stolen."

COFFEE TABLE BOOK CLUB

THIS MONTH'S SELECTIONS.

THE **PAPER CLIP**

by Esther Finnigan

Page after page of gorgeous photographs containing our most beloved office supply.

$79.00

HARRY L. MICHAEL'S

Aluminum Siding

A handsomely produced tome of glossy photos of America's most beautifully "'sided'" homes.

$99.00

Ed & Jeanine Baker's

MEALS 1985

No recipes, no commentary. Just full-page, full-color photographs of every meal eaten by the Bakers in 1985.

$129.00

R. Chast

ROZ CHAST

"Your editor at Random House
has been summarily fired and he
wants to take you with him."

BRIAN SAVAGE

PC. VEY

PETER VEY

INFLUENCES

SIDNEY HARRIS

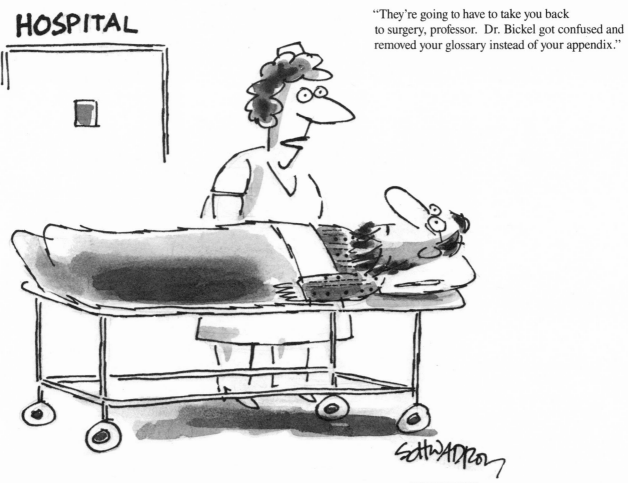

HOSPITAL

"They're going to have to take you back to surgery, professor. Dr. Bickel got confused and removed your glossary instead of your appendix."

HARLEY SCHWADRON

EVERETT OPIE   © 1968 The New Yorker Magazine, Inc.

"No, I haven't read the New Testament, but I read the Old Testament,
and I liked it very, very much."

THE FINE LINE BETWEEN FACT AND FICTION

RICHARD ORLIN

JONIK

JOHN JONIK

NOW
THE STORY CAN
BE TOLD!

WHY
I
CROSSED
THE
ROAD

MEET THE
AUTHOR

DOUGHERTY

DON DOUGHERTY

"Honey, it's way past your bedtime.
Let's just read the Library of Congress description."

MICHAEL TWOHY

"It took me three years to smuggle this out, and it's been rejected
by every publishing house in the West."

BRIAN SAVAGE

"I read the book. I liked it. Then I saw the Picture. Now I don't like the book."

BORIS DRUCKER

A NOTE ON THE TYPE

This book was set on the linotype
in Parbleu, a recutting made directly
from type cast from matrices made
bjy the Fjenjjmjn, Rjjj Parjjjj. Thj jjjj jj jj jjceljjjj
jjjjjle
jjjj vort vort vortvort.
Eunice if you are reading this, I
love you. Hugs and kisses from
Lance at the Book Bindery,
Woonsocket, R.I.

SALE

ZIEGLER

JACK ZIEGLER

I think I'm finally coming out of my postmortem slump."

MICHAEL TWOHY

CHARLES ADDAMS

"Mr. Fortner isn't in today — would you like *me* to reject it?"

JOHN JONIK

BRIAN SAVAC

"Listen, a writer isn't always writing when he's writing."

"Would you have that in hardcover?"

ARNIE LEVIN

"We don't drink — we read. Do you have any good books?"

ARTEMIS COLE

OLIVER CHRISTIANSON (REVILO)

"He says he'll definitely get back to you between the last dissonant dying chirp of the cicada and the first winey snap of the new frost air."

DONALD REILLY

"This man's name happens to be Ichabod Crane, and he wants to know if it's too late to sue the estate of Washington Irving."

ERRATUM

The illustration on page 462 labelled 'cow' actually depicted the Battle of Hastings. The correct illustration is shown here:

COW

SIDNEY HARRIS

OLDDEN

DICK OLDDEN

ARTISTS & WRITERS BAR

EDITORS & PUBLISHERS BAR

PRINTERS & TYPESETTERS BAR

SUBSCRIBERS AND READERS BAR

HENRY MARTIN

"I checked out *Gone With the Wind* in large type."

MICHAEL TWOHY

PETER PORGES

LEE LORENZ

"A writer? Fantastic! I wish I had time to write."

"I wonder if the 'Harvard Classics'
are still up there. Yep, there they are."

CHARLES SAXON

BERNARD SCHOENBAUM

"I'll take it. Charge it to Beatrix Potter's account."

S. GROSS

SAM GROSS

"No, I've never read *Rememberance of Things Past*,
but I've got the t-shirt."

EDWARD FRASCINO

STUART LEEDS

"It was the best of times;
it was the worst of times..."

JOHN JONIK

"Well, I haven't actually *read* it, but I've Walkmanned it."

DONALD REILLY

EDWARD FRASCINO

"You've probably never heard of him. He won the Pulitzer for poetry."

AROUND THE BEND
by Marnie Dobbins Dorne

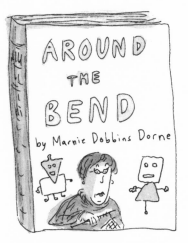

In this book, Ms. Dorne tells us about the aliens who visit her only when she is knitting.

OFF OF ONE'S ROCKER
by Henry Radishworth, III

Mr. Radishworth's careful accounting of all of his past lives, with special emphasis on his incarnations as Napolean, Sherlock Holmes, Cleopatra, Freud, Leonardo, and Madame Pompadour.

MELINDA C. SARNOW'S
BATS IN MY BELFRY

Ms. Sarnow's adventures along the time-space continuum which, as everybody knows, runs through her apartment.

R. Chast

ROZ CHAST

"The latest work in James McMurphy's oeuvre is a pretentious and ill-conceived exercise in maudlin sentimentality burdened by a turgid and plodding prose style, a forgettably pedestrian plot, and feeble-minded attempts at wit...."

O'NEILL   CATHARINE O'NEILL

ART HISTORY PHILOSOPHY NON-BOOKS

S. GROSS

SAM GROSS

BILL WOODMAN

"Have some consideration. There are people downstairs trying to write a book review."

MORT GERBERG

"Ladies and gentlemen, boys and girls, children of all ages — The Literary Lions!"

MICHAEL MASLIN

MICHAEL TWOHY

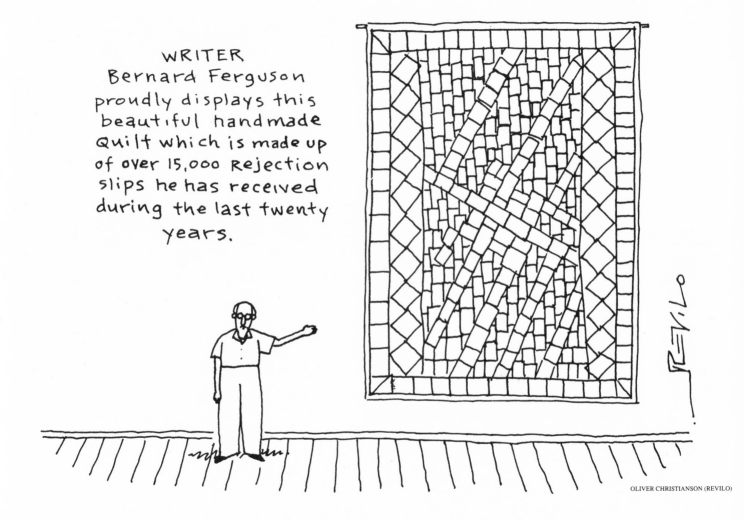

WRITER Bernard Ferguson proudly displays this beautiful handmade Quilt which is made up of over 15,000 Rejection slips he has received during the last twenty years.

OLIVER CHRISTIANSON (REVILO)

BILL WOODMAN

ADVERBS
25¢

EUGENE MYERS

"It's after Labor Day. We've come to collect your summer reading."

SAM GROSS

"I love my novel, don't you?"

CATHARINE O'NEILL

LEO CULLUM

"Sorry. I'm still under the influence of Hemingway."

FELIPE GALINDO (FEGGO)

NOVEL   NOVELETTE   NOVELLA   NOVELEENY

MICHAEL CRAWFORD

© 1984 The New Yorker Magazine, Inc.

PETER STEINER

How about 'this book is dedicated to my editor, Milton Fenderman, whose patience, sage counsel, and unwavering faith made it happen'?"

Man who's made his pile
and now wants to help others make
their pile thus making his pile bigger.

ELDON DEDINI

PETER PORGES

JACK ZIEGLER

"This is the Main Street Bookshop. The copy of 'Nature's Way to a Two Week Face Lift' you ordered has come in."

GEORGE BOOTH

ROZ CHAST

R. Chast

"You know who's beginning to annoy me? *Homer!*"

AL ROSS

TIM HAGGERTY

"It's a short story about a woman who wants desperately to write a novel but doesn't have the time."

WOODMAN

BILL WOODMAN

ELDON DEDINI

"No more for me, Joe."

EVERETT OPIE

"Add a little more scarlet."

SAM GROSS

SUBTEXT

P. Steiner

PETER STEINER

"Truscott Farnsworth III and his brilliant though as yet unpublished memoirs."

WARREN MILLER

© 1983 The New Yorker Magazine, Inc.

"You'll like this one, sir — it has a surprise ending in which the murderer turns out to be the detective."

ALEX NOEL WATSON

Period magnified five hundred times.

BERNARD SCHOENBAUM

EVERETT OPIE   © 1978 The New Yorker Magazine, Inc.

"We rather fancy this little novel of yours, Brown. Would you consider
one million six up front for it?"

"This ought to teach them a lesson."

BILL WOODMAN

LEE LORENZ

"Mr. Kellwood is looking for someone to assist him in recasting his journals into a form suitable for a wider audience. The tone should be urbane, warm and scholarly — somewhat in the manner of Lewis Thomas, but, of course, about plywood."

"The evening was delightful, Mona, and it's given me a wonderful idea for an epic novel."

EDWARD FRASCINO

WRITER'S BLOCK

Temporary

Permanent

T.ROGER CLAYPOOL'S FISH STORE

© 1983 The New Yorker Magazine, Inc.

SIDNEY HARRIS

MICHAEL MASLIN

"I'm sorry, but our only copy of *Yourself and Future Self* was just checked out."

PETER PORGES

"I've got an idea for a story: Gus and Ethel live on Long Island, on the North Shore. He works sixteen hours a day writing fiction. Ethel never goes out, never does anything except fix Gus sandwiches, and in the end she becomes a nympho-lesbo-killer-whore. Here's your sandwich."

BOOTH

GEORGE BOOTH

Man discovers the very three books with which he would have chosen
to be stranded on a desert island.

BERNARD SCHOENBAUM

"I plagiarized it because I thought it bears repeating."

NURIT KARLIN

"Dear Aunt Frieda:
     Thank you very much for the large book . . ."

CHARLES SAXON

D.W. SMITH
PUBLISHER

ED ARNO

"You call this The Great American Novel? It's in Hungarian."

SAM GROSS

"Now aren't you glad I talked you into using a pseudonym?"

PHIL INTERLANDI

"It's her last wish upon retiring after twenty-five years."

DON OREHEK

LIZA DONNELLY

P.C.VEY

PETER VEY

"Hey! This is the same book I read last vacation."

"And just what kind of jacket did you have in mind?"

BERNARD SCHOENBAUM

CRY, THE BELOVED COUNTRY CLUB

MICHAEL CRAWFORD

CHARLES SAXON

"But I can't send it back to Bryn Mawr College library after
twenty-eight years with a nice note."

JACK ZIEGLER

MICHAEL MASLIN

"You have to find the do-it-yourself books yourself."

SAM GROSS